Study Guide for
The Re-Forming Tradition

D1711723

Volumes in the Series

The Presbyterian Presence:
The Twentieth-Century Experience

The Presbyterian Predicament:
Six Perspectives

The Mainstream Protestant "Decline":
The Presbyterian Pattern

The Confessional Mosaic:
Presbyterians and Twentieth-Century Theology

The Organizational Revolution:
Presbyterians and American Denominationalism

The Diversity of Discipleship:
Presbyterians and Twentieth-Century Christian Witness

The Pluralistic Vision:
Presbyterians and Mainstream Protestant
Education and Leadership

The Re-Forming Tradition:
Presbyterians and Mainstream Protestantism

Study Guide for
The Re-Forming Tradition:
Presbyterians
and Mainstream Protestantism

By
Milton J Coalter
John M. Mulder
Louis B. Weeks

Westminster/John Knox Press
Louisville, Kentucky

Book design by Denominational Resources

First edition

Published by Westminster/John Knox Press
Louisville, Kentucky

This book is printed on acid-free paper that meets the American National
Standards Institute Z39.48 standard. ∞

PRINTED IN THE UNITED STATES OF AMERICA
9 8 7 6 5 4 3 2 1

Library of Congress Cataloging-in-Publication Data

Coalter, Milton J.
  Study Guide for The re-forming tradition—Presbyterians and
mainstream Protestantism in the twentieth century / Milton J.
Coalter, John M. Mulder, Louis B. Weeks. — 1st ed.
      p.   cm.
  Includes bibliographical references.
  ISBN 0-664-25411-X (pbk. : alk. paper)

  1. Coalter, Milton J.   The re-forming tradition.   2. Presbyterian
Church—United States—History—20th century.   3. United States—
Church history—20th century.   I. Mulder, John M., 1948–   .
II. Weeks, Louis, 1941–   .   III. Coalter, Milton J.   Re-forming
tradition.   IV. Title.
BX8937.C63 1992 Guide
285'.1—dc20   92-12543

Contents

A Personal Introduction

"How can our adult class study it?" That was the response from several Presbyterian ministers and elders who read the manuscript of *The
Re-Forming Tradition*. This guide offers several ways of helping adult
groups in church school classes, sessions, and retreats learn together
from our work. We here try to highlight some of the major themes of
each chapter and offer some suggestions to spur discussion. We also
identify additional resources that may be helpful.

The three of us who guided the project are Presbyterians who worship in Presbyterian congregations. We also work at Louisville
Seminary to teach those who lead congregations and serve God in other ways. We are Christians first, and we believe the Christian faith includes many other ways of being faithful—a rich Eastern Orthodox tradition, Roman Catholic perspectives that affirm today many emphases
of the sixteenth-century Reformation, and other Protestant affirmations
that have roots in scripture and sustain the church.

We undertook our study of the Presbyterian Church (U.S.A.) because we love it. It nourished us, and it still does. We think that if the
Presbyterian Church (U.S.A.) is able to grow in faithfulness and mission, the whole of the Christian community benefits. More important,
if our Presbyterian Church hears the gospel and proclaims it with clarity, God is glorified. In the final analysis, that is why we all worship
and serve.

In this study guide we speak particularly to Presbyterians. We hope
you will read and benefit from our efforts. We hope our research will
prompt you to learn more about your own congregation and its particular identity and mission. We also hope you will learn about and become more a vital part of the wider church—the Presbyterian Church

(U.S.A.), the hundred or so partner churches with which we have special work, and the universal Church to which we belong.

One of the historic marks of Presbyterians is our willingness to confront complicated and difficult issues. The problems and the opportunities before us today are complex. We know the Holy Spirit works among us to provide clarity and discipline so that we can make good use of learning. We count on that as we now lead you through some of the ways you can make use of *The Re-Forming Tradition*.

If you confront difficulties in your planning, please call one of us. We are also teachers, and we constantly lead groups in learning. We have asked a number of Presbyterian ministers and other teachers to make themselves available from time to time to speak about the study to classes and groups of churches. One or more may live close to you. We may even be able to suggest other resources as you focus the results of our study on the particular needs of your church.

Joe Coalter
John Mulder
Louis Weeks

Part I:
The Re-Forming Tradition:
Presbyterians and
Mainstream Protestantism

1

Looking Backward:
Religion and American Culture

This chapter provides the setting for our study of the Presbyterian Church. We look at American culture and the broad trends in American history. These present the backdrop for the particular developments within Presbyterian life that later chapters describe.

Major Themes

A. Disestablishment. In the fourth century the emperor Constantine recognized Christianity as the Roman Empire's official religion. Churches were given special privileges by the state. European countries kept some kind of established or legally recognized Christianity for centuries. This pattern continued in many early American colonies. A first disestablishment of the privileged place of a church occurred in North America when the U.S. Constitution provided for freedom of religion in the new nation. No one church would officially receive preferred treatment. But informally, Presbyterians and other "mainline" Protestants enjoyed generally favored relationships with American governments at all levels. A second disestablishment occurred in the early twentieth century when immigration from southern and eastern Europe—and later from Central and South America, as well as Asia—brought a sharing of favor and power among Catholics, Jews, and Protestants.

A third disestablishment is happening now. The first disestablishment was legal separation of church and state; the second disestablishment deposed mainstream Protestantism from religious predominance; the third increasingly separates the church and even belief from the culture itself. These three disestablishments have displaced American Presbyterians from their previous location at the center of the nation's cultural life.

B. Civil Religion. Historically, Americans have applied to the nation images borrowed from the Bible and the church of Jesus Christ. Sometimes these images—"a city set on a hill," for example, or "God's chosen people"—have been employed to speak of American responsibility; but more frequently they have been used to argue that Americans have special privileges and a unique mission. The early development of civil religion and some changes in the relationship between American civil religion and mainstream Protestant churches during recent decades are sketched.

C. The Division of Evangelical Protestantism. Early nineteenth century Protestants cooperated through a host of single purpose benevolent societies to create churches and Sunday schools on the frontier, to publish Bibles and religious tracts, to undertake foreign mission, and to promote social reform. Although from different denominations, participants were united in a shared evangelical piety which included Sabbath observance, regular family Bible study, devotional life, and worship, and were alike in the hope of forming a Christian America. During the remainder of the nineteenth and early twentieth centuries, this coalition divided over questions of social reform, the consequences of scientific discoveries, and the interpretation of scripture. Some Protestants tried to adapt their theology and practice to these new developments. Others considered such adaptations to be corruptions of Christian belief. Most Presbyterians tended to follow the first path, though Presbyterians were deeply divided as a smaller but vocal part condemned that path.

D. The Transformation of Modern America. There are changes that have "modernized" American life: urbanization; burgeoning immigrations; bureaucratization; increasing complexity in business, government, and education; the growth of ethnically distinctive populations and their interest in preserving their own particular cultures; expanding individualism and claims to personal rights; the development of the sciences; and the emergence of modern universities.

E. All these ingredients have worked together to make Americans more secular in their public life and more fragmented in their social identity. Religious belief is considered a private matter of personal preference, rather than a primary allegiance of people. This fragmentation is the setting for examining the re-forming of Presbyterian life and witness.

Helps for Discussion

1. Ask about changes in America that members of the class have experienced in their lives. Where were people born and where did they

grow up? What do they remember about schools, government, and business in their earlier lives? In a Cincinnati congregation, one older member talked about Presbyterian revivals, the help she received from the church when her family needed it during the Depression, and her ambivalence about women becoming elders in the 1940s when her church began to ordain them. This sets the atmosphere for all to talk about the situation in which Presbyterian churches live today.

2. Ask about their parents and grandparents and great-grandparents. What do participants remember about the religious practice of these relatives—their Bible study, Sabbath observance, church attendance, etc. This is a good way to lead into a discussion of their own history. Ask them to keep recollections brief and to the point. Tell them the purpose is not just to tell stories about family but to learn about the complicated and personal nature of change.

3. Take one of the sections you consider important and show a portion of the text—for example, the section on "The Compartmentalization of America." Ask members of the class to give illustrative examples from their own lives. This will help people see the application of the learnings early in the sequence, and it will help them see how each paragraph contains ideas for use.

4. Try to balance coverage of the chapter with attention to those parts most helpful for your group, or for the congregation as a whole. In later chapters we will return to many of these themes. You will have other chances to look at these themes regarding Presbyterians.

5. We strongly suggest you begin and end each session with prayer. As you will see, the development of spiritual disciplines will be an important conclusion of this study, and you can practice during these study times an important point to be learned from this research. We have found members who will gladly share prayer leadership if asked in advance. (If your group or class is accustomed to opening and closing with prayer already, rejoice!)

6. Ask a different class member each session to bring and read a brief passage of scripture that speaks to the situation to be considered that day.

2

Whither the Mainstream Protestants? Membership Growth and Decline

Major Themes

A. Membership loss has been significant. Since 1965, Presbyterian membership has declined by one-third. In addition, Presbyterians have been losing members relative to American population growth since World War I. The subject is a complicated one, however, and membership figures are difficult to compare.

B. Many factors have contributed to this loss. Declining birthrates, divisions and schisms, and changing American life-styles all had an impact. Presbyterian growth and decline patterns were closely tied to birthrates. But other factors internal to the church contributed significantly.

C. Membership loss is not primarily a defection of Presbyterians to more conservative churches. More people drop out of all church involvement than leave to fundamentalist churches. Although conventional wisdom has frequently blamed the "liberal" positions of the Presbyterian Church on matters of race and gender for the loss, we find that more people leave the Presbyterian Church to be of "no religious preference" than to join more conservative churches. The Presbyterian Church gains more members from more conservative denominations than it loses to them.

D. The Presbyterian Church has not increased in its percentage of African American, Hispanic, or Native American members over the last twenty-five years, although the American population has grown in all these racial ethnic minorities. Only among immigrant Korean populations has there been a marked increase in the number of members of the PC(USA), and many of those came to the United States as Presbyterians.

E. The so-called baby boomers, those born between 1945 and 1965, offer special challenges for churches. The expansion of the Presbyterian churches in the 1950s happened in part because the parents of baby boomers brought them to church. Presbyterians have lost a great number of those baby boomers who were reared in the church. Baby boomers raised in other denominations have not joined the Presbyterian Church in large numbers either. The children of inactive "boomers" are in jeopardy, since past trends indicate that those who grow up without church affiliation do not usually join later in life.

F. Several kinds of nonmember participants in Presbyterian churches also offer opportunities for enlistment. If the people who identified themselves as "Presbyterians" actually belonged to the church, the size of the PC(USA) would more than double.

Helps for Discussion

1. Ask members to reflect on their own religious pilgrimage. How many were born in and grew up in Presbyterian churches? In most congregations, a minority of members did so. What brought members to the Presbyterian Church? This discussion can open issues of switching, denominational allegiance, and membership.

2. Ask group members to reflect on the spiritual journeys of their own families as another way to enter the conversation on membership. Together, you might look at the roll of a 1950s or early 1960s confirmation class in your congregation. Ask whether those people listed are in the church today. These concrete ways of entering discussion make the subject a real one. On the other hand, your own experience as a family or a congregation might differ greatly from the overall patterns.

3. Ask "How important is membership?" Presbyterians in recent decades have not stressed what membership means. We have made it very easy to enter and to leave a congregation. What happens in your congregation when a member ceases to come for several Sundays in a row? Is it noticed? If so, how do you let the absent member know he or she was missed? Is there a regular plan to visit people and listen to their issues and needs?

4. Remember that chapters 5–9 will suggest some ways of helping your congregation and the whole church respond to dilemmas of membership. At this point, let people talk freely about themselves and their families and membership issues for the church. After one such discussion in a New Jersey session retreat, a longtime member said, "This is the first time I've felt permission to express my own ambiguity regarding church membership. After all, Jesus called us to follow him. Now I can think more clearly about asking people to join our church."

3

The Organizational Revolution: Denominationalism and Leadership

Major Themes

A. In America, Presbyterian congregations started before the denominations. Unlike those European Presbyterian churches which were established by governmental acts, American Presbyterian denominations grew out of the cooperation of already existing congregations usually organized by missionary pastors.

B. Denominations in America were an experiment in the relationship between church and state. They allowed different Christian groups to tolerate one another and live free from interference from the state. In their early years, American denominations borrowed and adapted practices and institutions found elsewhere in American life to serve spiritual purposes. They "invented" theological seminaries, church-related colleges, Sunday schools, new funding patterns for mission, and many other aspects of current church life that we take for granted today.

C. Organizations changed radically. In the late nineteenth century, business, government, education, and other American institutions became more complex organizations. The Presbyterian denominations changed as well. To engage in mission overseas and in frontier areas at home, to serve the Sunday schools and programs for women, men, and young people, the denominations set up departments and bureaus of all kinds. These offices were managed by highly visible leaders skilled in organization and administration.

D. Organizational complexity at all levels of Presbyterian life required leaders with administrative skills. This altered the priorities among Presbyterian ministers, even at the local level. Along with the traditional duties of preaching and providing pastoral care, the pastor assumed responsibilities for management and administration. The pastor became in effect the Chief Executive Officer (C.E.O.) of the church, and the session assumed duties similar to those of a board of directors for a corporation. "Higher levels" of church government likewise rewarded leaders more for their management skills than for their spiritual gifts and charisma, though many leaders continued to have both.

E. Members of this increasingly "corporate" church assumed the roles of passive stockholders, investing their funds and their time in the church but gradually feeling somewhat alienated from the decision-making of the denomination and even the congregation.

Helps for Discussion

1. Start by looking at the organization of your congregation when it began. If the church is a relatively old one, ask some longtime members to describe what they remember of developments in previous decades. You may see evidence of how the church increased in complexity as time passed. If your church is quite new, you can look at the ingredients in its beginning. Look at your presbytery as well. How has its mission changed and its complexity increased?

2. Bring a copy of the *Minutes of the General Assembly of the Presbyterian Church (U.S.A.), Part I: Journal.* Look for the numbers of committees and for their composition. Committees have usually been listed in the last few pages, and the index can help you see how many diverse responsibilities there are. Pass the book around so everyone can peruse it as you talk about organization. It can also help you talk realistically about the current organization of the denomination. (Another aid is the Presbyterian Planning Calendar, which lists the various ministry units and personnel of the church. Both are probably in the pastor's study or the church office.)

3. Discuss the similarities and differences between the church, both locally and denominationally, and the businesses in your community. How have businesses changed and adapted to new situations? What of their methods do you see incorporated into your congregational life? Which of their methods seem appropriate for the congregation?

4. Look at the budget of your particular church. Compare it with an older budget, one from the 1960s or even the 1950s. What percent of the budgets goes and has gone to current expenses, presbytery, synod, and General Assembly? If there has been a change, ask why that change occurred for your church.

4

The Predicament of Pluralism:
Theology and Confessions

Major Themes

A. Presbyterian theology has changed as the church confronted the challenges of the modern world. In the nineteenth century, Presbyterians paid careful attention to the Westminster Confession of Faith and the catechisms that accompanied it. Toward the end of the nineteenth century, and in the early decades of the twentieth, theologians, pastors, and members grew quite uncomfortable with the seventeenth century statements about God, Jesus Christ, the Holy Spirit, the Bible, and the relations of God with the church and with humanity. New theologies emerged which sought to supplement or replace the Westminster Standards as major emphases for most Presbyterians.

B. Both old and new theologies tried to be true to scripture. Presbyterians have consistently studied the Bible in light of new biblical scholarship and new situations in the world.

C. Presbyterians decided not to be fundamentalist. The 1927 PCUSA General Assembly refused to require all of its ministers to accept what fundamentalists considered the five "fundamental" doctrines of the Christian faith. Instead, the Assembly depended on presbyteries to determine the orthodoxy of their ministers. Since the fundamentalist controversy, Presbyterians have tended to define themselves in terms of what they are not—not fundamentalist—rather than by what they do believe.

D. Neo-orthodoxy, which took both the Bible and the modern world seriously, offered for many Presbyterians a basis for consensus after World War II, at least for a while. But it offered a better critique of earlier theologies than a basis for a commonly shared theology or interpretation of scripture. Most theologians have moved to other emphases more recently.

E. The new Brief Statement of Faith is grounds for hope that Presbyterians can proclaim a shared theology. But much more conversation about God and scripture needs to occur among Presbyterians in their congregations. In addition, Presbyterians must seek an identity rooted in their theological beliefs and affirmations.

Helps for Discussion

1. Ask members of your group to write down on a piece of paper two or three of their most important theological convictions. Then discuss their lists of doctrines in light of the chapter. Your group may agree closely on theology, especially if you are in a small church or if your group has been studying theology together previously. Most of the time, though, comments will be very diverse. In a North Carolina church, we heard some say "freedom," "sovereignty of God," "Jesus loves me," and "representative leadership." These would probably be typical responses of Presbyterians in a city church. We then asked each person to explain how the belief that they identified worked out in his or her own life and in the church. The lesson of pluralism today was made by the participants in the class.

2. Bring some copies of the *Book of Confessions* of the PC(USA) and talk about its contents. See how some of the confessions address obvious issues of today. See how others seem addressed to quite different times. Ask about the importance of confessions. Should people learn them by heart? All of them? Which do members already know? Did they learn others? Should children learn catechisms?

3. Ask members of the group to talk about their use of the Bible. Ask about changes in worship and preaching in your particular church. How has the use of the Bible changed in recent years? How seriously are members of the congregation studying the Bible? In what setting do their studies take place? In what ways do they interpret their beliefs to others?

4. Name a situation and ask for theological help: "A friend asks you, 'Who is Jesus Christ? Is he alive? What proof do you have?'" or "You try to comfort someone whose husband died. What do you say?" Have responses changed over the past decades?

5

The Varieties of Witness:
The Debate Over Evangelism

Major Themes

A. During the nineteenth century and the first decades of the twentieth, Presbyterians tried to evangelize people in the United States and abroad. Schools, medical assistance, care for the poor, ministries of justice, mission with immigrants, and other helping institutions were seen as ways of spreading the message of Jesus Christ and inviting people into the membership of the church.

B. During this century, we have split the education and care of people (our outreach through service) from our verbal explanations of our Christian motivation for helping (our verbal outreach). We have identified evangelism with judgmental and offensive intrusions into other people's business. We associate evangelism with televangelists, fundamentalists, and other very conservative Christians. We avoid conversations about what we really believe with friends, family, business associates, and sometimes even with other church members we are afraid of offending. Denominationally, we have also diminished our efforts to create new churches in areas of population growth.

C. This has happened at the same time that an increasing number of people do not know of Jesus Christ or do not find the Christian Church addressing their spiritual needs. Colleges and universities, which were once places where people frequently heard about and joined Presbyterian churches (or rejoined, if they had grown up Presbyterian and left briefly as they matured), now offer scant opportunity for thinking people to find a thinking faith, such as Reformed Christianity has offered. College ministries have in most cases dwindled in size, outreach, and financial support. The denomination's presence in the public forum of radio and television has been drastically reduced.

D. Many Presbyterians have come to see evangelism as being opposed to social witness and ministries of peace and justice. Things that once went hand in hand are now seen as competitors by many. Presbyterians see these two activities as either/or, although they used to see them as both/and. We need to recover the mutually reinforcing relationship between evangelism and social witness.

Helps for Discussion

1. Ask members of the group to talk about their normal conversations with friends, family, and associates. Do people they come in contact with know that they are Christians? Do those they help know they help because they are Christians? In a group one of us taught, a woman described succinctly a commonly preferred method of outreach among Presbyterians today. She said: "I prefer to live my faith and circulate!" This woman is a very articulate English teacher, one who teaches others to express themselves well with words. But her statement suggests that "living" the faith does not include using words to express the faith. Is this position characteristic of your church community?

2. Discuss the two verses from the Sermon on the Mount: "Let your light so shine . . . " and "Beware of practicing your piety before others . . ." (Matt. 5:16 and 6:1). Do we pay careful attention to both? Does one way of being a Christian predominate among us?

3. Ask each member of the group: "What brought you to the Christian community?" Ask members: "What brought you to this church? Why do you stay? What do you believe?" Then ask when was the last time they were asked these questions outside of a session meeting when they joined the church. Discuss how we can express our faith outside our church home if we have seldom (or never) done it in our own church family.

4. What procedures and practices does your church follow to welcome and invite visitors to join your congregation? Does anyone host or "shepherd" visitors on Sunday mornings? Does anyone call on visitors by phone or in person? How much of the early contact with visitors is done just by the paid staff?

6

The Diversities of Discipleship: Mission, Racial Ethnic Ministries, Ecumenism, and Social Justice

Major Themes

A. The evangelical character of the Presbyterian churches in the nineteenth century prompted great interest in foreign mission. As churches took hold in various lands, American (and European) denominations gradually surrendered their power to dictate the structures and theological perspective of newer churches. Partnership in global mission has replaced the older ways of sending missionaries, who superintended churches elsewhere in the world.

B. Similar changes have occurred with ministries among Native Americans, African Americans, Hispanics, and Asian Americans. Where previously it was generally assumed that minorities ought to absorb the practices and culture of the majority, the call of the gospel is now seen to require people to be inclusive of other cultures and of minority interests and representation. The support of distinctive Christian emphases and cultures requires new skills and dedication on the part of all Presbyterians.

C. The movement toward multicultural Presbyterian life offers great opportunities for church members to teach each other the multiple emphases of the Christian gospel. In this new situation, Presbyterians can witness to all parts of the American population. But the reality is that members of all the major racial ethnic minorities in the Presbyterian Church experience severe demands and considerable ambiguity. Most try to remain faithful to their own racial and ethnic sensibilities and heritage. They also try to engage in work and worship with other minorities and with the Anglo majority. Conflict between these two efforts arises and makes evangelism, education, and even worship difficult when the Anglo majority assumes that the denomination simply should reflect its culture and heritage.

D. The ecumenical movement has triumphed. Protestant churches and other Christian bodies in the United States and elsewhere now collaborate as never before. The movement has even brought some, albeit limited, organic union among denominations. But the ecumenical attitudes of Americans in general and Presbyterians in particular have meant the eclipse of some distinctive elements in Presbyterian heritage. People ask, "Why bother with denominations at all?" The challenge now is for Presbyterians to regain a sense of what distinguishes them from other members of the Christian family so they may again make a unique contribution to the wider, ecumenical body of Christ.

E. Presbyterians have always worked for social reform, but the agenda of issues has changed. The loss of the "Sabbath" as a major part of Presbyterian witness has meant, for example, that we do not focus on the ways personal and corporate piety undergird and sustain social witness. The number of issues on the denominational agenda has also increased, and the methods for assuring compliance have moved increasingly toward seeking legislation, sometimes pitting those at regional levels against those in local churches. Presbyterians have spent less time and energy and fewer resources for the education of members and officers in the nature and demands of the Christian life. At the same time, the PC(USA) suffers intractable conflict as a part of a larger American "culture war" that encourages single-issue politics and limited institutional loyalties.

Helps for Discussion

1. Look at your support of global mission. Does the congregation give for the support of a particular missionary? for several? Who are they? What do they do? Compare this situation with that of previous decades in the life of the congregation—say, before World War II. Are you "receiving" missionaries now? This is a good way into discussion on mission.

2. If your congregation is primarily African American, Hispanic, Native American, or Asian American (whether Korean or from other peoples in Asia), you will want to refer to the particular essay regarding your history in the PC(USA). See the volume *The Diversity of Discipleship: Presbyterians and Twentieth-Century Christian Witness,* chapters 8–13. If your congregation is predominantly "white," you will need to learn more about these Presbyterian sisters and brothers.

3. If your group contains members of Presbyterian racial ethnic minorities, ask them to speak concerning their ambivalence (if any) in participating in a predominantly "white," Anglo denomination. Our figures show that many areas of America already contain a majority of peoples of color. What does this mean for the outreach of your congregation?

4. Ask people about the religious affiliation of their neighbors. Discuss the local ecumenical movement in your town or city, or in your area of the country. Are Presbyterians at the core of it? Who shares leadership? Do people who receive aid ecumenically know why Christians are working that way? Do they realize that local social agencies are Christian at all?

5. A woman in Florida at a "Presbytery Day" said, "We Presbyterians must think we are saved by respectability! Our major value seems to be 'Give no offense.'" How do you appraise this statement?

6. When you discuss the social witness of the Presbyterians, remember that almost all of us think some involvement in the cultural, social, and political life of the community and the nation is important. For almost all of us, the question is the kind of social action and for what issues we get involved. We guarantee a lively discussion on this topic!

7

The Ecology for Nurturing Faith: Education, Disciplines, and Programs for Faith Development

Major Themes

A. Churches at their best create an ecology, or ecosystem, of practices and institutions that nourish faith. Among Presbyterians this has consisted first of family gatherings for Bible reading and prayer, and the dedication of Sundays for public worship and nurture. Other institutions—congregational worship, Sunday schools, church-related colleges, theological seminaries, church camps, women's, men's, and youth groups, and many others—have together provided a web of support and training in the Christian life. The Holy Spirit has developed and nourished faith through these interdependent institutions and rituals.

B. The denominational ecosystem is in serious disrepair. Researchers in our project find all the parts of the web of support radically changed—some entirely gone, some severely diminished, and still others intact but carrying heavier burdens because of the absence of their partner institutions. Most Presbyterian families, for example, do not have frequent, regular times for reading the Bible and praying together. Aside from attending Sunday worship, few Presbyterians practice Sabbath observance and refrain from work, commerce, or entertainments. A diminished church school struggles to compensate for gaps in the Christian nurture of children and adults in the home. Colleges and seminaries have become much more pluralistic, less interested in cultivating distinctly Presbyterian leaders.

C. Presbyterian programs of nurture need attention and renewal. In some cases, old practices and institutions should not be resurrected, but new alternatives are needed to replace their functions. There have been changes in recent decades in Presbyterian publishing houses, denominational journals, women's and men's groups. The parts they played in the ecosystem are discussed.

D. Presbyterians have creatively changed the ecosystem before, and they need now to revitalize their ecology with a mutually complementary set of formal and informal institutions. Such institutions can help new generations have faith and vibrant Christian life. We do not believe, of course, that this is only a human work. God is about this work even in our current situation. A man in a congregation in Texas, hearing about this part of our study, observed: "I'm a trustee at a Presbyterian college. I see my job as to bolster that college, support its finding ways to feed the faith of young people. And I need to devote myself to Bible reading and prayer about that task, while I pray for others doing other jobs that complement it." He caught the spirit of what this chapter tries to explain.

Helps for Discussion

1. Ask members of the group to tell about their growth in faith. What part did family devotions and Bible reading play in their religious experience? Were there special patterns to their family's life on Sunday? How does your church try to augment the efforts of members and families to read the Bible devotionally and regularly? Pray, as the Bible says, "without ceasing"? Enjoy the depth and power of corporate worship? In groups that we have taught, we have seldom gotten beyond this topic because of the intense interest of many people in it. Nor have we wanted to, for if we Presbyterians are able to engage effectively in devotional Bible reading and prayer, we will see how God intends us to weave a web of support for faith for tomorrow's world.

2. Bring in, if you can locate them, bulletins from worship services in previous decades. Alternatively, ask older members with Presbyterian backgrounds to talk about worship, Sunday observance, and other parts of Christian life in early decades of the century. The purpose is not to lament the loss of habits and institutions gone by, nor to gloat in the new freedom we have, but rather to see what functions these practices potentially played in Christian nurture and to discuss alternatives serving the same purpose and appropriate for us today and tomorrow.

3. Take the opportunity to learn about church-related colleges and campus ministries in your synod and about theological seminaries

in the PC(USA). We at Louisville Seminary are delighted to respond when people ask about us and the community here. We know other seminaries and church-related institutions would be equally happy to provide information about their mission and programs. You can find a list of both kinds of schools in the back of the Presbyterian Planning Calendar.

8

The Presbyterian Predicament:
A Case of Conflicting Allegiances

Major Themes

A. Christian discipleship involves several sets of dual allegiances. Each pair of allegiances has a complementary relationship. We describe several parallel allegiances that we think are important for Presbyterians. On occasion, Presbyterians have affirmed one so strongly that the other has suffered. Too much of one can cause the loss of a complementary responsibility and result in an incomplete discipleship. The diagram below is a visual scheme of the allegiances we describe in the chapter and the dangers if one is exaggerated to the exclusion of its partner.

1. **Biblical authority** ◄─► **Social relevance**
   (danger: fundamentalism)   (danger: secularism)

2. **Salvation of individuals** ◄─► **Redemptive transformation of culture** (danger: in the struggle for social righteousness, individuals' need for redemption is overlooked)
   (danger: Band-Aid redemption of individuals while social evils flourish)

3. **Verbal witness** ◄─► **Outreach through service**
   (danger: a loud noise signifying nothing)   (danger: a "Cheshire cat" witness, invisible since no one knows the Christian motives behind the service)

4. **Participatory democracy** ◄─► **Executive decisions**
   (danger: loss of cohesion)   (danger: dictatorial rule and decisions without a following)

5. **Distributed leadership** ◄─► **"Charismatic" leadership**
   (danger: leaders without followings)   (danger: guru worship)

    6. Reform through   ◄───►**Reform through legislation**
      education (danger: studying   (danger: harming voluntary
      too long with no action)   relations by coercion)

    7. Congregational integrity ◄───►**Connectional allegiance**
      (danger: group   (danger: corporate
      individualism)   regimentation)

    8. Ecumenism   ◄───►**Denominational identity**
      (danger: loss of identity)   (danger: parochial division of
                     the Church catholic)

B. Two examples from the diagram: In the eighth parallel allegiance, a close-knit, sectarian religious body might present a clear denominational identity by imposing strict limits on members' beliefs or by emphasizing the leadership of a particularly charismatic person. But a denomination such as the PC(USA) balances the need to maintain its own distinctive theological identity and piety against the desire to contribute its insights to the ecumenical church family and learn from contact with other distinctive Christian traditions. Likewise, in number five, Presbyterians wish to place those with God's charisma in leadership positions. But we also strive to distribute leadership lest individuals have unbridled power. In each case, too much attention to one of the parallel allegiances distorts the basic equilibrium. Correcting imbalances means seeking balance rather than elimination of an allegiance.

C. We compare the church to a mobile, a work of art that depends on balance among its parts for beauty. God's gift in Christ and the work of the Spirit make a plumbline, a center of spiritual gravity, for the Presbyterian Church as it seeks to balance priorities and loyalties.

Helps for Discussion

1. Try to discuss one of the sets of parallel allegiances in depth, rather than trying to spend equal time on all of them. The most important and perhaps the most difficult to comprehend and follow is the first—balancing biblical faithfulness and modern relevance. "Be in the world but not of the world" makes Christian sense, coming from the Bible itself (see 1 John 2:15–17). But the playing out of that balance challenges all of us all the time. Simple, personal illustrations from your life will help others make the connections.

2. Ask members of the group to describe their church's relationship to the denomination. Where have group members had contact with the presbytery, synod, or General Assembly? What were their impressions of these contacts? You might ask a member of the church who has been heavily involved in a presbytery committee (or had more extensive involvement) to enter into the discussion.

3. Ask members what they think distinguishes the Presbyterian Church from other denominations in the Christian family. Is there a reason for having denominations? Do all denominations seem similar? What are the real differences?

4. Ask where members of the group perceive the congregation to be out of equilibrium. What about the presbytery? the Synod? the General Assembly? How can balance be restored, if it is not present?

9

The Re-Forming Church:
An Agenda for Reform

Major Themes

A. We call Presbyterians to seek the re-forming of the church with repentance, in the Bible both a motion of turning away from and a motion of turning toward—away from our idols and toward God, away from old ways and toward ways of the gospel. Our repentance today means "confessing that we have distorted the meaning of the Christian faith and the church's mission. In accenting some part of the biblical message, we have failed to understand and proclaim the breadth of God's word" (p. 247). In repentance, we also see that God gives grace, grace to surrender previous animosities and to seek opportunities for service and witness.

B. We invite Presbyterians to focus on evangelism—speaking and acting the faith so others are invited to share the knowledge and experience of God's love through Jesus Christ. To do this, Presbyterians will have to "turn" away from their preoccupation with decline and growth in congregations and focus on the needs of those around them. In some cases, your congregation will have to concentrate its outreach and service on a particular constituency in your community. Not all the challenges can be met at once.

C. We propose three particular groups of people for concentrated PC(USA) efforts: "mental members," who already identify themselves as Presbyterian but do not belong to a church; the children of the baby boom generation; and members of American racial ethnic minorities. We give the reasons for our selection of these groups in the chapter.

D. We suggest that there is a rhythm to the healthy Christian life which involves faith, service, and witness. Each is essential, and all are present in equal measure to undergird the Christian experience.

E. As a denomination, the PC(USA) needs to give careful attention to new church development, ministries of various kinds on college campuses, and media ministries. All three have been important in the past but have been ignored in recent decades. In each, the church needs to experiment with new ways of accomplishing these ministries, challenging Presbyterians to use their creativity and energy constructively.

F. We invite Presbyterians to read the Bible and pray with more discipline and care. In families, this is critical for the growth of children in Christian faith. But we all grow enormously in faith and life with regular devotions and study.

G. We suggest ways for congregations, governing bodies, and leadership to be more effective. All need to be interested in nurture and less preoccupied with protocol and control.

H. We challenge all of us to recover a vital, common vision as well as to continue in friendly conversation about the important matters where we differ. We live in a Western world where the fastest growing "religious preference" is "no preference." In concrete terms, we have anguished over the person or family who left to join a fundamentalist church and ignored the eight or ten who walked out the back door to "no religious preference." We have fought among ourselves, while idolatries of money, power, and prestige have flourished. We need to recover our perspective, which puts God first and accepts no other as God.

I. We are convinced that God is not finished with Presbyterians. God still has a purpose for us. So let's get to it!

Helps for Discussion

1. This chapter is especially complex, and you may want to divide the various sections into separate sessions for the class. If you have only one session for it, you may choose to concentrate on the part most pertinent for your group or your congregation. Frankly, we debated long and hard about which conclusions from the fifty-five essays to include here. Our dialogues with church people in various parts of the country gave us more food for thought. We cut and edited to make one chapter of our various conclusions. You might copy the chapter outline and ask which topics are especially compelling, spending your time on those.

2. Let these conclusions suggest ways your group or congregation can "re-form" its witness and work. We dearly hope they will.

3. Ask people in the group what they would most like to tell us, and then have someone write us a letter. We will be happy to hear, and we will certainly respond.

4. One presbytery studying an earlier volume in the series began an action committee to try out some of the ideas in several of the essays. Such a plan might work for your group or congregation after reading this book. Alternatively, if your church has good working committees, you might make some referrals of things you learned and possibilities that exist for you.

5. If different members of the class have been opening and closing the sessions with prayer, you might now ask for sentence prayers as you conclude the study.

Part II:
The Presbyterian Presence Series: Essays and Authors, with Brief Annotations and Study Questions

1. The Presbyterian Predicament: Six Perspectives

1. "The Restructuring of American Presbyterianism: Turmoil in One Denomination," by Robert Wuthnow. Examines the Presbyterian struggle between conservatives and liberals and draws some implications for the future. How do you characterize your own stance as a Presbyterian? the faith of others in your congregation? How can Presbyterians become more faithful?

2. "The Presbyterian Heritage as Modernism: Reaffirming a Forgotten Past in Hard Times," by Edward W. Farley. Names six important and attractive theological marks of the Presbyterian Church today. How do you respond to these questions? What about other members of your congregation? Is this the Presbyterian heritage you want to pass to another generation?

3. "Uncharted Territory: Congregational Identity and Mainline Protestantism," by Barbara G. Wheeler. Develops a typology of theories for the study of congregations and calls for serious congregational studies among Presbyterians. What is the special history, identity, and mission of your congregation? What ways of studying the congregation seem most fruitful to you?

4. "On Dropping the Subject: Presbyterians and Sabbath Observance in the Twentieth Century," by Benton Johnson. Traces the decline of Sabbath observance and wonders how Presbyterians can recover a sense of sacred time. How important is "Sabbath" for you and

those around you? Are there other, regular characteristics of your Christian commitment that also function as "Sabbath" has?

5. "Identity and Integration: Black Presbyterians and Their Allies in the Twentieth Century," by Gayraud S. Wilmore. Detects changes in the nature of the ambivalence experienced by Black Presbyterians and calls on Presbyterians to transcend current expressions of that ambivalence. What does this history mean for your life and the lives of those near you? What are the most significant special pressures on and elements in the identity of African American Presbyterians today?

6. "Ministry of Word and Sacrament: Women and Changing Understandings of Ordination," by Barbara Brown Zikmund. Outlines the history of ordination, and locates Reformed ordination of women and its implications. What does ordination mean to you and to others in your congregation? Is the ordination of women affecting our theology? In what ways?

2. The Mainstream Protestant "Decline": The Presbyterian Pattern

1. "Numbering the Presbyterian Branches: Membership Trends Since Colonial Times," by Donald A. Luidens. Examines the complexity of membership numbers and what trends of growth and decline really are. What learnings from the membership figures can help the church most? How is church membership related to Sunday school participation in your congregation?

2. "Enhancing Church Vitality Through Congregational Identity Change," by Grayson L. Tucker. Presents results from self-studies by more than 250 congregations, with practical implications for renewal. Offers the image of a healthy congregation as one with two strong arms—mission and evangelism—and a strong heart of worship. What signs of health and disease do you find in your congregation? How does your church engage in mission, evangelism, and worship?

3. "Closing the Back Door: Toward the Retention of Church Members," by Donald P. Smith. Presents nine hypotheses drawn from a study of "conserving" churches, congregations successful in retaining members. How does your congregation work to retain members? What can you do to help?

4. "Denominational Defection: Recent Research on Religious Disaffiliation in America," by C. Kirk Hadaway. Discusses three kinds of nonmembers, from study of demographic patterns. How do you reach out to believers-not-belongers in your neighborhood? in your community? Which kinds seem most interested in sharing church life?

5. "The New Voluntarism and Presbyterian Affiliation," by Jon R. Stone. Presents a study of "nonmember participants" in California and their values. Are there nonmember participants in your congregation? Why won't they join? What can be learned from this analysis for your congregation?

6. "Membership Decline and Congregational Identity in Yonkers, New York: A Case Study in the Presbyterian Church (U.S.A.)," by Mark N. Wilhelm. Studies the self-perceptions of four congregations, relating their identities and their histories. What seems most important in the history and life of these Yonkers churches? What can be applied to your congregation?

7. "Reaching Out: A Study of Church Extension Activity in Mecklenburg Presbytery, North Carolina, 1920–1980," by Jerrold Lee Brooks. Shows how and why new church development was important in the Charlotte area before 1967 and how it has been neglected in recent decades. What is the comparable history for your presbytery? What significant efforts are underway now? How can you help?

8. "Mirror for American Protestantism: Mendocino Presbyterian Church in the Sixties and Seventies," by R. Stephen Warner. Follows shifting vitality, leadership, and theological orientation of one California congregation, as it moved from decline to renewal. How did the different leaders affect the congregation? How do leaders in your congregation care for it and help it flourish?

3. The Confessional Mosaic:
Presbyterians and Twentieth-Century Theology

1. "Pluralism and Policy in Presbyterian Views of Scripture," by Jack B. Rogers and Donald K. McKim. Studies the ways Presbyterians understood the authority and interpretation of scripture and how

these issues affected their understanding of major issues. Which ways of using the Bible seem most appropriate to you? How is the Bible used in your family? in your congregation?

2. "Redefining Confessionalism: American Presbyterians in the Twentieth Century," by James H. Moorhead. Finds redefinition of Presbyterian denominations as "confessional" churches. In what ways do you use Presbyterian confessions? How can they be most helpful in Christian growth? Is the idea of confessions appropriate and relevant for you and the church?

3. "Changes in the Authority, Method, and Message of Presbyterian (UPCUSA) Preaching in the Twentieth Century," by John McClure. Investigates the fluctuating authority, methods, and messages of preachers. What is the authority of the preacher? What methods make the most sense today? How do, or should, preachers use the Bible?

4. "Themes in Southern Presbyterian Preaching, 1920 to 1983," by Beverly Ann Zink. Finds common threads in sermons of PCUS preachers through the century. What themes pervade the preaching you hear (or the preaching you do)? Have these themes changed? In what ways? What themes seem most faithful to scripture?

5. "Challenging the Ethos: A History of Presbyterian Worship Resources in the Twentieth Century," by Ronald P. Byars. Describes the growing interest in liturgy and diverse worship forms among Presbyterian denominations. How has worship changed in your congregation? How do you interpret Presbyterian worship when you invite other people to join you for church? teach children in your congregation? incorporate new members?

6. "Hymnody: Its Place in Twentieth-Century Presbyterianism," by Morgan F. Simmons. Assesses the hymnals of the Presbyterians in light of modern trends and Reformed theology. What is the hymnody of your congregation? How can you and others in your church grow in Christian devotion through music? What music should be included in your church? Why?

7. "The Language(s) of Zion: Presbyterian Devotional Literature in the Twentieth Century," by Mark A. Noll and Darryl G. Hart. Follows the development of a new language of spiritual life alongside a more

traditional one. What is the language of your devotion? What written aids help you in your spiritual life? What aids do other members use?

8. "From Old to New Agendas: Presbyterians and Social Issues in the Twentieth Century," by Benton Johnson. Explores change and continuity in the goals and methods of Presbyterians seeking to transform culture. What should the social agenda of the PC(USA) be today? How can you support the church in its concentration on that agenda?

9. "The Tie That No Longer Binds: The Origins of the Presbyterian Church in America," by Rick Nutt. Examines the causes of division in the PCUS which led to the new denomination. What lessons can be gained from this history of division and separation? What should be the relationship of the PC(USA) to the PCA and other Presbyterian or Reformed churches?

4. The Organizational Revolution: Presbyterians and American Denominationalism

1. "The Incorporation of the Presbyterians," by Louis B. Weeks. Traces the local and national development of the formal, complex church of today with its benefits and costs. Did this happen in your own congregation? When? Why? What are your expectations concerning church personnel and programs?

2. "Managing the Mission: Church Restructuring in the Twentieth Century," by Richard W. Reifsnyder. Studies the purpose, patterns, and costs of major denominational restructuring efforts. How does denominational life affect you and your congregation? How do you and your congregation view the governing bodies of the PC(USA)? What can be done to bring these governing bodies and congregations together when they differ?

3. "The American Presbytery in the Twentieth Century," by Lewis L. Wilkins, Jr. Finds that the development of different kinds of presbyteries produced a transformation in the idea of mission. How does your presbytery engage in mission? What changes can you detect in its organization and its work over recent decades? How can its structure be improved?

4. "A Financial History of American Presbyterian Giving, 1923–1983," by Scott Brunger and Robin Klay. Describes changes in giving patterns and levels of financial commitment. How much

should Presbyterians be giving to the church? What about tithing and proportional giving? How can you and others in your church grow and help others grow in Christian stewardship?

5. "Changing Priorities: Allocation of Giving in the Presbyterian Church in the U.S.," by Robin Klay. Studies the movement toward local priorities for mission giving over time. What are the benefits and what are the costs of concentrating increasingly on local mission and program?

6. "Global and Local Mission: Allocation of Giving in the Presbyterian Church in the U.S.A. and The United Presbyterian Church in the U.S.A., 1923–1982," by Scott Brunger. Also notes the growing tendency toward economic localism in financial allocations by congregations. Do these figures also reflect your congregation's allocation of funds? What differences and similarities seem most important?

7. "A Financial History of Presbyterian Congregations Since World War II," by D. Scott Cormode. Explores why congregations increasingly spend more locally or designate their funds, rather than provide unified support for denominational mission. How does your congregation spend its money? How does your present budget compare with those two or more decades ago (if the church has been in existence that long)? How do you account for the changes in budget items? What should your church budget reflect by way of mission and care?

8. "Money and Power: Presbyterian Women's Organizations in the Twentieth Century," by Joan C. LaFollette. Describes the changes in control and program as women's organizations have been absorbed into denominational structures. How have Presbyterian women's organizations affected your life and the lives of those close to you? What roles can they play today?

9. "Men and Mission: The Shifting Fortunes of Presbyterian Men's Organizations in the Twentieth Century," by Dale E. Soden. Follows the development and the eclipse of vital men's organizations. What part have Presbyterian men's organizations played in your Christian formation? in your congregation's life? What roles and missions are appropriate today?

10. "Special-Interest Groups and American Presbyterianism," by Gary S. Eller. Relates the history and character of denominationally

approved special-interest groups and the debate concerning their role in denominational structures. Do you participate in special-interest groups? What special-interest groups seem appropriate among Presbyterians? What place should they have in church structure?

11. "The Emerging Importance of Presbyterian Polity," by David B. McCarthy. Shows that theological issues have been decided increasingly on the basis of polity. In what ways is theology polity for Presbyterians? What issues are significant for Presbyterian theology today? How ought they to be resolved?

12. "The National Organizational Structures of Protestant Denominations: An Invitation to a Conversation," by Craig Dykstra and James Hudnut-Beumler. Asks if the denominational structures have waned as resources and become increasingly structures that rely on regulation. Does this analysis ring true for you? What resources and what regulations of the PC(USA) have special importance for you? What can you do to provide nurture and resources for fellow Presbyterians and for other Christians?

5. The Diversity of Discipleship: Presbyterians and Twentieth-Century Christian Witness

1. "Presbyterian Evangelism: A Case of Parallel Allegiances Diverging," by Milton J Coalter. Studies the nature of Presbyterian evangelical roots and the recent split between verbal and social witness. How do evangelism and social witness fit together for you? What does the Bible say about their relationship?

2. "Twentieth-Century Presbyterian New Church Development: A Critical Period, 1940–1980," by Robert H. Bullock, Jr. Shows how and why Presbyterians have neglected new church development in recent decades. How did your congregation begin? What relationships has your congregation had to new church development efforts elsewhere? What does new church development today mean to you, your congregation, and your presbytery?

3. "The Rise and Fall of Presbyterian Official Journals, 1925–1985," by James A. Overbeck. Demonstrates the divisions among Presbyterians regarding the nature and purpose of the church and its official publications. How much freedom should editors of church

publications possess? How can you and your congregation support Presbyterian publications? What should they report or emphasize?

4. "A Poultice for the Bite of the Cobra: The Hocking Report and Presbyterian Missions in the Middle Decades of the Twentieth Century," by John R. Fitzmier and Randall Balmer. Follows the transformation in global mission as new churches become partners in ecumenical witness. In what ways do you and your church support global mission? What is the relationship of Christianity to other world religions?

5. "American Presbyterians in the Global Ecumenical Movement," by Theodore A. Gill, Jr. Argues that Presbyterians have been extremely important in the development of ecumenical movements worldwide. What major shifts do you perceive in Presbyterian global ecumenism? What differences do ecumenical commitments make in local Presbyterian congregations?

6. "Presbyterian Ecumenical Activity in the United States," by Erskine Clarke. Traces the ebb and flow of domestic Presbyterian ecumenical involvement. In what ways do you and your congregation embody Presbyterian ecumenism? Are there limits to ecumenical involvement? What are the benefits and costs of ecumenical activity?

7. "Presbyterians and Mass Media: A Case of Blurred Vision and Missed Mission," by J. W. Gregg Meister. Examines Presbyterians' early involvement in mass communications and their later discomfort with and retreat from the public arena of mass media. What media are most appropriate for proclamation of the gospel? How can your congregation make use of media for mission and evangelism?

8. "A Presbyterian Dilemma: Ecclesiastical and Social Racial Policy in the Twentieth-Century Presbyterian Communion," by Joel L. Alvis, Jr. Describes the church's shift from a policy segregating African Americans from "white" membership to a policy of integration and subsequently of seeking the self-development of peoples. What is the status and nature of this dilemma today? What resources exist for overcoming the dilemmas of race in American life and in church life?

9. "Identity and Integration: Black Presbyterians and Their Allies in the Twentieth Century," by Gayraud S. Wilmore. Detects changes in the nature of the ambivalence experienced by Black Presbyterians

and calls all Presbyterians to transcend current expressions of it. In what ways have Black Presbyterians changed in organization and emphases? What special contributions do Black Presbyterians bring to the whole denomination?

10. "Native American Presbyterians: Assimilation, Leadership, and Future Challenges," by Henry Warner Bowden. Discusses the history of Presbyterian concern with Native American missions and the dilemmas now faced by Native American Presbyterian leaders. How does Native American theology relate to Euro-American Christian Presbyterianism? What can the rest of us learn from Native American Presbyterians?

11. "Hispanic Presbyterians: Life in Two Cultures," by Francisco O. García-Treto and R. Douglas Brackenridge. Examines three major segments of Hispanic Presbyterianism: Mexican American, Puerto Rican, and Central American. What similarities and differences exist among the three segments of Hispanic Presbyterianism? How do their experiences resemble those of other "racial ethnic minorities"? How can their unique cultural perspective broaden our understanding of the church and of the gospel?

12. "Contexts for a History of Asian American Presbyterian Churches: A Case Study of the Early History of Japanese American Presbyterians," by Michael J. Kimura Angevine and Ryô Yoshida. Explores the ambivalence of Japanese American Presbyterians torn among competing allegiances. What special needs and gifts have Japanese American Presbyterians brought to the rest of the church? What should be done in the future?

13. "Korean American Presbyterians: A Need for Ethnic Particularity and the Challenge of Christian Pilgrimage," by Sang Hyun Lee. Examines the fastest-growing component in American Presbyterianism, calling for a multicultural church of fellow pilgrims. In what ways can all Presbyterians be pilgrims? What examples do Korean Presbyterians set for the rest of the church?

6. The Pluralistic Vision: Presbyterians and Mainstream Protestant Education and Leadership

1. "The Predicament of Pluralism: The Study of Theology in Presbyterian Seminaries Since the 1920s," by John M. Mulder and

Lee A. Wyatt. Shows the evolution of the seminaries as the Princeton theology was replaced by a host of competing perspectives. Should there be a "core" of Presbyterian theology? What should be the central affirmations of the Presbyterian Church? How should they be taught in seminaries?

2. "Nurseries of Piety? Spiritual Formation at Four Presbyterian Seminaries," by Steve Hancock. Traces the increasing pluralism of Presbyterian piety and the increase in programmatic responses to the perceived needs of seminary students. Can prayer and spiritual life be taught? How? What activities or programs help the most?

3. "Presbyterian Colleges in Twentieth-Century America," by Bradley J. Longfield and George M. Marsden. Shows the increasing secularism in a steadily decreasing number of church-related schools. What special role should Presbyterian colleges have in higher education? What has "church-related" meant and what does it mean today?

4. "Presbyterian Campus Ministries: Competing Loyalties and Changing Visions," by Ronald C. White, Jr. Assesses the growth and decline of emphasis on campus ministries among Presbyterians. How does your congregation relate to college students? What ministries do you provide? What ministries do you collaborate with others in presbytery to offer? How can they be strengthened and improved?

5. "Presbyterians and Their Publishing Houses," by John B. Trotti and Richard A. Ray. Studies the development of denominational publishing houses and the increasing demands upon them. What is the special responsibility of Westminster/John Knox Press? How independent should a press be editorially? financially?

6. "A Brief History of a Genre Problem: Presbyterian Educational Resource Materials," by Craig Dykstra and J. Bradley Wigger. Shows how teaching faith was replaced by teaching a curriculum in Presbyterian church schools. How do you "teach your faith" to others? Is the person of the teacher more important than the curriculum? If so, what does this mean? Through what curricula do you and others in your congregation learn?

7. "The Use of the Bible in Presbyterian Curricula, 1923–1985," by David C. Hester. Considers the place of scripture in Presbyterian

educational materials, and shows the increasing complexity required for teaching as historical-critical methods have been intro-
duced. How is the Bible used in your Christian education program? Which ways of using the Bible seem particularly appropriate for Presbyterians?

8. "Changing Leadership Patterns in the Presbyterian Church in the
United States During the Twentieth Century," by Richard W.
Reifsnyder. Provides a group biography of southern Presbyterian
leaders. What experience and what Christian gifts are characteristic of Presbyterian leaders?

9. "Transformations in Administrative Leadership in the United
Presbyterian Church in the U.S.A., 1920–1983," by Richard W.
Reifsnyder. Gives a parallel study of PCUSA, UPCNA, and
UPCUSA leaders, showing growing demands for managerial
skills. How does this group biography compare with the previous
one (chapter 8)?

10. "Looking for Leadership: The Emerging Style of Leadership in the
Presbyterian Church (U.S.A.), 1983–1990," by Richard W.
Reifsnyder. Assesses the selection process and the General
Assembly leaders of the new denomination. Who are the leaders
of our church? How are denominational leaders encouraged and
supported by your congregation? How are you and other
Presbyterians you know cultivating future leadership for the
church?

11. "Presbyterian Women Ministers: A Historical Overview and Study
of the Current Status of Women Pastors," by Lois A. Boyd and R.
Douglas Brackenridge. Discusses the historical barriers to women
becoming ministers and the difficulties they continue to face in being accepted as church leaders. What barriers remain for women
ministers? How has the ordination of women affected your own
personal experience and your congregation's life?

12. "Cleavage or Consensus? A New Look at the Clergy-Laity Gap,"
by Keith M. Wulff and John P. Marcum. Studies similarities and
divergence of views of Presbyterians on a variety of issues. Have
"gaps" inhibited or assisted mission? In what ways? How can
these divisions be healed or bridged?

13. "The Values and Limits of Representation and Pluralism in the Church," by Barbara Brown Zikmund. Explores the need for both inclusivity and a common identity among Presbyterians. In what ways does Presbyterian inclusivity affect your worship and work? What limits to pluralism make sense to you?

Order the *Study Guide for The Re-Forming Tradition: Presbyterians and Mainstream Protestantism* and other valuable books:

Presbyterian Publishing House
*A division of Publications Service
Presbyterian Church (U.S.A.)*
100 Witherspoon Street
Louisville, Kentucky 40202-1396

or call toll-free
1-800-227-2872
Monday through Friday
9:00 to 4:30 Eastern Time

ORDER HERE
(all volumes are paperback)

Please send me the following books in quantities noted:

The Presbyterian Presence:
The Twentieth-Century Experience series—

_____ The Confessional Mosaic:
Presbyterians and Twentieth-Century Theology
#025151X0 **$14.99**

_____ The Diversity of Discipleship: Presbyterians
and Twentieth-Century Christian Witness
#025196X0 **$16.99**

_____ The Mainstream Protestant "Decline":
The Presbyterian Pattern
#02515010 **$12.99**

_____ The Organizational Revolution:
Presbyterians and American Denominationalism
#02519780 **$16.99**

_____ The Pluralistic Vision: Presbyterians and
Mainstream Protestant Education and Leadership
#02524350 **$15.99**

_____ The Presbyterian Predicament: Six Perspectives
#02509710 **$12.99**

_____ The Re-Forming Tradition:
Presbyterians and Mainstream Protestantism
#02529900 **$16.99**

_____ Study Guide for The Re-Forming Tradition:
Presbyterians and Mainstream Protestantism
#025411X0 **$ 2.99**

Other books of interest—

_____ Sealed in Christ: The Symbolism of the Seal of the
Presbyterian Church (U.S.A.), *by John M. Mulder*.
   (Examines the facets of the seal: cross, dove,
   fish, book, pulpit, cup, fire, and triangle.)
   #18091004   **$ 4.95**

_____ To Be a Presbyterian, *by Louis B. Weeks*.
   (Offers a clear and concise introduction to
   what it means to be Presbyterian.)
   #00001880   **$ 6.99**

_____ The Presbyterian Source: Bible Words That Shape
a Faith, *by Louis B. Weeks*.
   (Explores the Presbyterian tradition, using the
   Bible as a guide.)
   #02510050   **$ 6.99**

Methods of payment:
Include 10% of order subtotal for shipping, $2 minimum, $20 maximum.

❏ **Check enclosed: $**_____

NOTE: $10.00 minimum on all charge orders

❏ **PPH Charge Account #**_____

❏ **Visa**   ❏ **MasterCard**
❏ **American Express**   ❏ **Discover**

Enter card number here: _____

Expiration date: _____

Interbank MasterCard: _____

_____
Signature (required for all charge orders)

SHIP TO:

_____
Name/Church

_____
Street address (necessary for UPS delivery)

_____
City, State, Zip code